D1508140

how happy is
your
Marriage?

50 Great Tips to Make Your
Relationship Last Forever

Sophie Keller

HARLEQUIN®

How Happy Is Your Marriage?

ISBN-13: 978-0-373-89250-1

© 2011 by Sophie Keller

All rights reserved. The reproduction, transmission or utilization of this work in whole or in part in any form by any electronic, mechanical or other means, now known or hereafter invented, including xerography, photocopying and recording, or in any information storage or retrieval system, is forbidden without the written permission of the publisher. For permission please contact Harlequin Enterprises Limited, 225 Duncan Mill Road, Don Mills, Ontario, Canada, M3B 3K9.

Author photograph by Sarah Corwin Photography

Library of Congress Cataloging-in-Publication Data

Keller, Sophie.

 How happy is your marriage? : 50 great tips to make your relationship last forever / Sophie Keller.

   p. cm.

ISBN 978-0-373-89250-1

1. Marriage. 2. Married people—Psychology. 3. Man-woman relationships.
4. Marital quality. I. Title.

HQ734.K367 2011

306.872--dc22

     2011010356

How Happy Is is a trademark of Sophie Keller.

® and TM are trademarks owned and used by the trademark owner and/or its licensee. Trademarks indicated with ® are registered in the United States Patent and Trademark Office, the Canadian Trade Marks Office and/or other countries.

www.Harlequin.com

Printed in U.S.A.

To Oli, the love of my life, without whom
I could never have written this book.

CONTENTS

INTRODUCTION

Imagine you are fourteen years old, in school and starting a new class called Marriage. In this class you learn fifty tips, and once you've learned them, for the remainder of time that you are in school, all you do in that weekly class is role-play the tips with your fellow students. That's it—there is no more new material to learn, because those fifty tips are all you need to know in order to make your relationship work. You spend the rest of your time in Marriage class studying the same tips and integrating them into your life to prepare you to make your future marriage work.

This book contains fifty definitive tips to help make your marriage last forever. I believe if we all learned each of these tips and put them to practice, there would be far more happy marriages.

As you read, you may notice that you've already mastered some of these tips, and you can check those off, but there will be others that you may not have thought of and that are completely new to you. If you invest in your relationship and master all fifty tips, the reward for a marriage that works will be higher than you ever thought possible and has the potential to bring you more joy than anything else in your life.

With a good marriage you need to always think, how will my actions now affect my relationship in an hour, in a day, in a month, in a year, in a lifetime? My general rule of thumb is that if what you do or say to your partner will affect your relationship in a positive way, then do it. If not, or if you're not sure, then think again about whether it is worth the temporary satisfaction.

To make your marriage work, you will need good listening skills, because half of what makes a happy marriage is being able to listen and respond to your partner. You will also want to be able to give to each other at every available opportunity, to come to agreements effortlessly and let each other flourish and be the best you each can be.

My husband, Oli, often tells a story about something that happened many years ago, when he was at friends' parents Liz and Hugh's thirtieth wedding anniversary. Oli was sitting next to Liz and watching Hugh's best friend, Steve, who was in his late fifties, dancing, kissing and flirting with a young blond bombshell that he brought with him to the party. Just six months earlier, Oli had seen Steve with another beauty, doing pretty much the same thing at another party.

Oli, who was in his early twenties at the time, said to Liz, "Wow, Steve is the coolest guy and such a stud. Whenever I see him, he's always with another really sexy, gorgeous woman."

Liz looked incredulously at Oli and said, "Oli, it's really easy to pick up another pretty girl, spend a few nights or weeks with her and keep her happy and satisfied for a short period of time. You want to know who really is the coolest guy in the room?" Liz pointed at her husband. "It's Hugh. Hugh has kept me happy sexually and emotionally for thirty years. A man who can keep a woman happy for that long is a real stud."

My goal with this book is to help you have a great marriage, too. So take your time, read the tips and, more important, practice them. They really do work. Take one at a time if need be, and work with that one for a week or a month and let it integrate seamlessly into your life and then move on to integrating the next. Invest time and attention into your marriage and you'll find that the rewards for doing so are really high. Your relationship will flourish and you and your partner will bring each other happiness for years to come.

Good luck, and let me know how it goes.

Love, Sophie

QUIZ: HOW HAPPY IS YOUR MARRIAGE?

Read each question and circle the answer that best applies to you and your relationship. If there are steps you can take to improve your relationship based on your answers, turn to the relevant tips in the book and start creating a happier marriage, one tip at a time!

Circle the answer that sounds the most accurate, then turn to page 105 for your results.

1. **What best describes your relationship?**

    A. Challenging, frustrating and slightly volatile. We often miscommunicate.

    B. Loving, communicative and happy. We are both growing together.

    C. Boring, withdrawn and somewhat disconnected. We are both a bit lonely.

2. **How do you both handle a disagreement or argument?**

    A. We listen calmly, acknowledge if our partner has a point and respond in a matter-of-fact way.

B. One or both of us bottle up our feelings and give the other the silent treatment.

C. One or both of us are loud, volatile and talk over the other all the time.

3. **Do you feel heard and completely understood by your partner?**

    A. On some things, yes, and others, no.

    B. I don't feel that I'm understood at all, and I have a hard time expressing myself to my partner.

    C. Yes, completely.

4. **How much does your partner really know about you?**

    A. I am keeping a lot of secrets and generally have a hard time sharing everything with my partner.

    B. I am really open and my partner knows everything about me.

    C. I have a few secrets that I am keeping from my partner.

5. **Do you find it easy to talk about sex with your partner?**

    A. We are fully open and find it easy to discuss.

    B. We don't discuss it; it is a bit of a taboo subject.

    C. One of us is open and the other more closed.

6. **Are you happy with the amount of sex that you are having with your partner?**

   A. No, I often want more.

   B. My partner wants more than me.

   C. We are totally happy with our sex life and have the amount that is good for both of us.

7. **Are you happy with the creativity and variation in your sex life?**

   A. There are things that one of us wants to do but that the other doesn't.

   B. Sometimes it gets a bit boring and we could spice it up.

   C. We are totally happy, open and compatible and have great sex.

8. **Do you spend a good balance of time together and apart?**

   A. We spend too much time together and stifle each other a little.

   B. The balance is just right; we have good quality time together and apart.

   C. We do not have enough time together.

9. If your partner does something to annoy you, do you:

   A. Tell your partner immediately that he has rubbed you the wrong way?

   B. Say nothing but remember it for an argument later on?

   C. Say something if it's really important and let it go if it isn't?

10. If your partner points out that you have done something to upset her, do you:

   A. Fight your point, just so that you can be "right" and turn it into something bigger than it really is?

   B. Get upset that she is upset and turn the attention back to you?

   C. Say you are sorry quickly and hope your partner will forgive you?

11. If your partner apologizes to you for something he has done, do you:

   A. Forgive him and move on pretty quickly?

   B. Lie to him and tell him it doesn't matter and he doesn't need to apologize, when it actually does matter to you?

C. Acknowledge his apology but still hold resentment toward him for days?

12. When your partner says something ridiculous in public, do you:

A. Apologize to the other people and tell them your partner can be misguided at times?

B. Stick up for your partner whether she is right or wrong, since, after all, she is your spouse?

C. Say nothing and discuss it with your partner privately later?

13. If you could give more to your partner, what would you give him more of?

A. My time and focus.

B. Physical attention and/or sex.

C. I am good about giving to my partner, both in terms of physical attention and in terms of time and devotion.

14. When you are in an argument, do you make empty threats about your relationship without meaning to?

A. Always.

B. Never.

C. Sometimes, just to get a rise out of my partner and see how she reacts.

15. **When you encounter difficult life obstacles, such as the loss of a job, loss of a loved one or a health crisis, do you find that:**
    A. It brings you closer together and you deal with it as a team?
    B. You question the validity of the relationship as the stress pulls you apart?
    C. You argue more?

16. **After being apart for the day, do you:**
    A. Barely acknowledge each other when you see each other?
    B. Kiss or hug hello the moment you see each other?
    C. Sometimes give a warm welcome and sometimes not?

17. **When your partner tells you that he wants to go away for a weekend by himself with a few friends, do you:**
    A. Try to get invited?
    B. Kick up a fuss since you don't want your partner to go?

C. Tell your partner to go and have a great time?

18. **Do you think you and your partner bring out the best in each other?**

    A. No, we argue a lot and encourage each other to live an unhealthy lifestyle.

    B. Sometimes we are good for each other and at other times we are not.

    C. Yes, we are better people together than we ever were apart.

19. **How many interests and hobbies do you share together, beyond bringing up kids, if you have them?**

    A. None.

    B. A few, but we would like more.

    C. We have plenty of common interests and hobbies.

20. **When talking to your partner, are you conscious of the kind of language that you use?**

    A. I don't usually think about it. I just say whatever comes into my head.

    B. I am conscious of the language I use and how I use it.

C. Yes, but I often say the wrong thing, in the wrong way, and unintentionally upset my partner.

21. **If you feel that your relationship has gone off course and you are growing apart, do you:**

A. Decide that things aren't as you want them to be, and address this by making sure that you go on dates together and spend good quality time by yourselves to strengthen your bond?

B. Think this must be a sign that the relationship is over?

C. Declare yourself helpless, since, after all, relationships change and yours is no different?

22. **If you have had a bad day at work, when you come home, do you:**

A. Try to pick a fight and act slightly passive-aggressive with your partner because you are in such a bad mood?

B. Bottle it up, withdraw from your partner and try to work it out for yourself?

C. Tell your partner what happened that day to get it out of your system and then drop your mood so you can have a nice night together?

23. **How well do you sleep together?**

    A. We are incompatible bed buddies; that is, one of us snores, fidgets or generally keeps the other awake.

    B. Some days are good; some not so good. But we cope.

    C. We sleep really well together and get the amount of rest we both need.

24. **As you spend more time with your partner, do you feel that:**

    A. Your relationship is going stale?

    B. You are evolving and growing together?

    C. You are temporarily growing apart but trust that you will grow back together without having to put much effort in?

25. **If you have kids, how often do you go out with each other alone, as a couple, on a romantic date?**

    A. Once a month if we are lucky.

    B. Maybe a few times a year or not at all.

    C. Once a week at least.

1 Treat Your Relationship like a Flower

A marriage is made up of two living, breathing human beings who are constantly changing and evolving. Your relationship is a balancing act, because both of you are in such a constant state of flux.

Like a flower, your relationship grows and blossoms in its own time and at its own pace. You can never push it to evolve faster, just as you cannot pull at the roots of a flower to make it grow. It takes great sensitivity, awareness, patience, listening and endless giving. And, like a flower, your relationship has its own set of seasons. At times it grows quickly; at other times, slowly. Sometimes there are droughts and its growth stalls, and other times it flourishes, attaining new depths with ease. You never want to under water it and you never want to overwater it.

You will learn more about yourself in a marriage than you ever will being single, as your partner holds a mirror up to you, revealing where you need to heal and grow. Trust in each other to teach one another. Together, you can be stronger and freer than you ever could alone.

2 Have the Right Amount of Sex

Relax. There is no right or wrong amount of sex in a marriage. Every couple is different and everyone needs different amounts of sex. So as long as you are both in agreement and satisfied with the amount of sex that you're having, you're doing well. Sex tends to be a taboo subject, and as with money, it is often considered rude or tasteless to ask how much people have. But sex is just another part of life; it is not something that we should be embarrassed to talk about. Many great couples that I know have sex three times a week or more and many have it less. Ideally, you want to be with a partner who wants similar amounts.

However, if both of you want different amounts, then you really need to talk about it so that you both get your needs met. Do you each feel comfortable having sex two times a week, three times, every day? A friend of mine said that she was at her church one day and the sermon was on sex. The priest said to his congregation, "My wife and I have sex three times a week. That's how much I like to have it and how much I need to have it. We are both really busy, so we have set days and times, which we have put aside to make sure that our needs are met. So after this service, for example, we are going to have sex. [Perhaps at this point he gave a little too much information!] But you all need to be clear on what your needs are and make sure that you are getting them met." (Of course, this sermon could happen only in California!)

If you are someone who finds it hard to talk about sex and your needs, then the best way to approach the conversation is to:

1. Be really clear about what you want. Perhaps that means taking a moment to write down your thoughts for yourself to clarify matters before you chat about them.

2. Choose a time when you are both relaxed and feeling close to speak about it. Avoid this discussion when one of you is rushing in or out or is in the middle of an errand.

3. Approach the conversation positively. Sex for some can be a very delicate subject. If you both discover that you have different needs and one of you wants sex five days a week and the other wants it once a week, then do your best to accept each other's desires and come to a healthy agreement that works for you both. Perhaps that means that you settle on twice a week every other week and three times a week every other week. You really do not want to blame

your partner if he or she has different desires than you. You both want to reach an agreement in order to accommodate one another's needs. The relationship is such an important part of your life that you both need to be prepared to make changes for each other.

4. Be open to discussing ways that you might bring more play and creativity into your sex life. This will help spice it up, and if one of you wants sex less often, this may encourage that person to be excited about having more.

5. Keep the conversation open and loving and allow your partner time to respond and express his or her opinion without interrupting.

Sex is, for most of us, an essential part of any relationship. Physical intimacy feeds your emotional, mental and spiritual intimacy as a couple. So even if you have children and you feel that your time is limited, you must still make time for sex. Your marriage is always going to be number one.

So don't shy away from talking about sex, make time for it and schedule it in if you need to. Be sure that your physical needs as a couple are being met!

3 Choose Your Battles Wisely

Choose your battles with your partner carefully. Don't pick on your partner for absolutely everything he does, as this will cause him to eventually stop feeling free around you. In marriage, it's essential to let the little things go!

When you do want to speak to your partner about something that bothers you, don't attack or blame him. Speak from your heart, and tell him how much it upsets you and why. If you come from a place of vulnerability, rather than anger, it's much more effective and less likely to cause an argument.

Think about giving feedback like you are making a sandwich. Start with something encouraging, such as a compliment for something your partner does really well, and then include the feedback, explaining what you want your partner to do differently in concise, nonjudgmental language. End with another compliment or positive comment. By layering feedback in a "sandwich," your partner won't feel attacked. Be gentle with your partner. If your partner feels appreciated, he is more likely to do what you want. Like the famous adage goes, "You catch more flies with honey than you do with vinegar."

4 Say You Are Sorry

If you've done something wrong, say sorry, and say it quickly. It takes the air out of any situation and saves you hours of battling over a point, which you sometimes forget about before the argument is even over.

Some people find it extremely hard to say sorry, even if they know that they have done something to upset their partner. This stems from a fear of being wrong and a desire to be right all the time.

If you feel that you are with a partner who finds it hard to say sorry and you find it easy, and you are in a situation where you really feel you have been wronged, then you are the one who will have to open up the "sorry" dialogue.

One way to do so is to say something like: "I am sorry that we argued. The last thing that I ever would want to do is upset you." Now, in this case the "sorry" word is out in the open, but you haven't lied or taken the blame and let your partner off the hook. This way you open up the dialogue for your partner to say sorry as well. That way no one has to compromise. Your partner can then more easily say sorry, too, and more often than not, the disagreement is over.

Most arguments that you have are logistical and mean nothing compared to the vision that you need to have for your relationship. Remember that you want your marriage to last a lifetime, so keep the big picture in mind when you go to apologize. If it feels disingenuous to say you're sorry, because you really don't want to admit guilt, then you can once again say something like, "I'm sorry that we argued." Then follow it with, "I really want what is best for us and sometimes we miscommunicate and that is upsetting." By presenting it this way, you are still using the *S* word, just not as directly, and without admitting blame.

If your partner is upset with you, then listen to what she has to say. Most likely she is upset for a good reason. Think about what you want in the long term and then decide if it's more important to be right or to say sorry.

5 Forgive

Just as it's important to apologize when you've done wrong, it's important to be openhearted when your partner apologizes. If your partner says sorry to you for doing something, forgive him. (Unless, of course, it's something that affects your core values within the relationship, such as having an affair.) There is no point wasting precious time holding a grudge. It's tiring, and the anger that you feel can only build up over time and cause damage to your relationship.

You have to give your partner the benefit of the doubt if he says sorry and really means it. If you did a survey, you would see that the people who really do have the best relationships tend to forgive each other very quickly. They argue, let it all out, forgive each other and then it's over.

If you are someone who holds on to something for days, stop it! Right now! It's not fair to the person you love. You can't make your partner suffer if he has said he's sorry. So stop being angry and hurt and let it go!

6 Disagree the Right Way

Disagreeing is healthy in a relationship. There is nothing wrong with it, so long as you are able to resolve your disagreement quickly and easily, without holding a grudge. Of course, you also don't want to be arguing all the time, as that is not the basis of a good marriage. But you can't be afraid to speak your mind, either. It is more about how you speak it than anything else.

I get concerned when couples don't have disagreements at all because I always wonder what they are holding on to inside and what is building up over time. I had a past boyfriend whom I didn't argue with at all, but it also wasn't a very passionate relationship and it eventually ended, ultimately because of what was not said. When you do disagree with your partner, there are ways to do it healthfully and productively.

Here are some tips to help you argue the right way:

Stick to the Subject

Steer clear of everything from the past. In a disagreement, bring up only what you are at odds about in that given moment, not something that happened three months ago. If you are dragging up old issues that you haven't gotten over, that is not healthy at all. It builds layers upon layers of anger and hurt and makes what you are disagreeing about too loaded to actually resolve, and as a result the argument can get out of control.

Keep Calm

Disagreements don't necessarily need to be heated. They can actually be conducted quite reasonably and nonemotionally if you try. If you both come to the table willing to come to an agreement, forgive and listen to one another, this is possible.

Sometimes you can agree to have different perspectives and not get upset and judge the other person for her opinion. The fact that we are all so unique and different is what makes the world such an interesting, diverse and creative place. So be more curious and interested in your partner's perspective, rather than critical or bothered by the fact that she thinks differently than you.

Put It in Perspective

Probably .0000001 percent of arguments are life-or-death situations. In fact, if you look back on them, most of your disagreements are probably about very little. A year later, will it matter if your partner didn't pick up his socks off the floor or didn't have time to make that grocery run? Even if you think back to last year and how many arguments you had, you probably have forgotten what most of them were about, because ultimately they probably weren't all that important!

So disagree if you must, but try not to do it all the time and move on from the small issues as quickly as you can.

7 Come to an Agreement Rather Than Compromise

Compromising is almost always one of those things that nobody wants to do, because it implies that you aren't getting exactly what you want. And yet often when you hear people talk about marriage, they talk about making compromises.

The word *compromise* has never sat well with me. It always seems a bit stifling and implies sacrificing my own needs for someone else's. So instead of compromising, I think of coming to an *agreement.* In the same way that the word *compromise* suggests taking away what I wish for, the word *agreement* suggests I am freely, of my own volition, coming to a decision with my partner that works for both of us. In making this decision, we take each other into account and our goal is to take what we both want and make it work for both of us.

Now, come on, doesn't that sound much more inviting than coming to a compromise? The next time you are having a disagreement, work toward an agreement, rather than a compromise, and you'll find you get there much more easily—and both of you will feel infinitely better about it.

8 Don't Play Therapist

No matter what your partner is dealing with, you never want to act as your partner's therapist, as it changes the dynamic of your relationship and sets it off balance. Of course, you will want to be supportive of your partner as he goes through trying times, but there's a difference in being a supportive spouse and acting like a therapist.

Giving your partner space to figure things out on his own and letting your partner know that he has your full support are two excellent ways to be supportive without playing therapist. You can even recommend a therapist if your partner is interested. It's also okay every now and then to give your partner advice in a lighthearted, nonjudgmental way, but only if he asks you for it. But when it comes to those deeper-rooted issues, let your partner look elsewhere. Because if you become your partner's shrink, the relationship can easily turn from one between lovers to a parent/child dynamic, which is hardly very beneficial for your sex life!

9 Always Be a Team

Never undermine your partner in public by exposing anything about her that's private, by criticizing her or, if she is having a dispute with someone, by taking the other person's side. Not only will you appear disloyal, but also this can actually undermine the strength of your relationship.

When you get married, you enter into a partnership—you become a team. In order to keep your union strong, you have to stick together as a team and work as a united front. If you don't agree with what your partner is saying in public (it happens in the best relationships from time to time!), just stay silent until you are asked to comment, and if you are, just say that your partner has strong opinions and has her own mind. You can always discuss your opinion with your partner in private afterward.

10 Don't Fall for Potential

Being in love with your partner's potential can be very dangerous. You need to be satisfied with who you married and who your spouse is now, not who you want him to be or what you think he is capable of. Loving someone's potential keeps you from seeing your partner for the wonderful person he already is and tempts you to put pressure on him to fulfill the goals that you have for him.

Maybe your partner is not capable of what *you* think he is capable of. For example, are you holding out for him to become more tactile or to hug you more? What happens if he never does? Maybe he organically expresses his love in different, less physical ways.

So instead of looking at what your partner could be, look at yourself and where you aren't meeting your own needs. Your partner doesn't need to reach for goals that *you* have set for him. People transform themselves because they want to, not because someone else wants them to. And when they do, they tend to do it in their own time and in their own way.

11 Be Giving

The most important question to ask yourself in the context of your relationship is, what can I give to it? rather than what can I get from it? This way you are sure to always strengthen your marriage.

One of the primary ways to make a relationship work is to give to the other person at every opportunity. Obviously you both need to be giving to each other so that your relationship is balanced. I am not saying to not take at all, but rather to always have the other person in mind with everything that you do.

It's so easy to make your partner feel loved and special and so important to do it as much as possible, with little things. For example, if your partner has had her hair cut, tell her it looks great. If you think she looks good in a particular shirt, make sure to tell her just how good you think she looks. Go out secretly and buy her her favorite chocolates, cook her favorite dish, massage her feet out of the blue, hold her hand at the movies. Notice what she does for you, thank her for it and give as much as you can to her as well. It's so easy to make each other happy. All you have to do is to think about the other.

When I was growing up in London, there was an advertising campaign for Nestlé Rolos, a chocolate and toffee candy, that has stuck with me. The tagline was, "Do you love anyone enough to give them your last Rolo?" In the commercial, giving your last Rolo to the one you loved was the ultimate sacrifice, and for some reason I think of that advertisement often. I do my best to give Oli my last Rolo, and in order to make your marriage last, that is what you both must do. And think about it—if you're both giving each other your last Rolo, then both of you benefit!

12 Judge Not, Lest Ye Be Judged

Don't judge your partner because he is different from you. Let him be himself without criticism. Criticizing will just cause hidden resentment that will build up over time and make you both unhappy.

No one is perfect and we all have our idiosyncrasies. You fell in love with your partner despite them, and perhaps even because of them! You must remember that you both had different upbringings, you have different genes and you may be from different cultures. One of you may be a single child and one of you may have seven siblings. You see the world through different eyes and have different ways of doing most things.

You wouldn't want to marry someone who is a replica of yourself. If you can already "do you" really well, why would you want your original self and a clone of yourself under one roof? With that in mind, give your spouse a break. Sometimes some of the differences we love when we first meet our partner turn into the differences that begin to annoy us over time. But do your best to remember back to when you first met your partner and found these differences endearing; in this way you can fall in love with them all over again.

My mom is a great example of this because she very rarely talks badly about my father. In the odd moment that she is upset with him, she may say, "Oh, I'm upset with Richard. He's being really stubborn." But in the very next breath she will say, "He's such a fine man!" Because she knows that his stubbornness is also what makes him so loyal to her and so stable.

In the same way, whenever you find yourself judging your partner, stop and focus on your partner's most positive attributes and what he is amazing at.

At any given time, you always want to be able to list ten amazing qualities about your partner, in quick succession. Think about ten things (or more!) that you absolutely love about him, and write them down (here or in another journal). Keep these at the forefront of your mind, and remind yourself of them when you are tempted to judge or criticize and hold your tongue. And, on occasion, when you are intimate together, remind your partner about all his amazing qualities. You will see that by doing this, you will make him feel exceptionally appreciated and will remind him of who he is. Also, you will find that the love and appreciation will come back to you in spades.

Ten Things I Love about _____:

----

13 Know Each Other's Primary Sense

Even though we all use all our senses, most of us have one primary sense or combination of senses through which we communicate. Understanding how you and your partner both express love can help you communicate more effectively and express yourself more clearly in your relationship. We all have five senses:

Visual: What You See

Auditory: What You Hear

Kinesthetic: What You Feel

Gustatory: What You Taste

Olfactory: What You Smell

Three of these—visual, auditory and kinesthetic—are the primary senses and each of us tends to favor either our seeing, hearing or feeling sense. (Taste and smell are less dominant, and don't play the same role in learning or communication.) We always use all senses at the same time, although we might not be equally aware of them and usually one is stronger and leads the others.

You can tell what your partner is just by listening to the words and phrases that he uses. For example:

A Visual Person

Someone who is primarily visual often uses words such as *look, focus, insight, perspective, outlook, show, reveal, illustrate, clarify* and *examine.* A visual person frequently employs phrases such as:

> *I see what you mean*
> *It appears to me*
> *We see eye to eye*
> *Show me what you mean*
> *The future looks bright*

A visual person communicates by seeing and doing. He expresses love by doing things for or with you. He feels most loved when you buy him gifts, make him dinner or do a chore for him.

An Auditory Person

Someone who is primarily auditory often uses words such as *say, resonate, sound, clear, discuss, tone, rhythm, listen, tell, shrill* and *harmonious.* An auditory person frequently employs phrases such as:

Rings a bell
Loud and clear
Music to my ears
Unheard of
Sounds good to me

An auditory person communicates by talking and listening. They express love by sharing thoughts and views with you. They feel most loved if you talk and communicate a lot with them and when you tell them how much you love and appreciate them.

A Kinesthetic Person

Someone who is primarily kinesthetic often uses words such as *touch, handle, pressure, stress, grasp, warm, gentle, concrete, tackle* and *heavy.* A kinesthetic person frequently employs phrases such as:

I will get in touch with you
Hold on a second
I can't put my finger on it
I can grasp that idea
I feel it in my bones

A kinesthetic person communicates through her body and loves physical activities. She expresses love by touching and hugging.

She feels most loved when you kiss her, massage her back, hold her hand or run your fingers through her hair.

Your primary sense says a lot about how you express and recognize love. For instance, I am a very feeling person and I am primarily kinesthetic. So when Oli holds my hand, massages my feet or puts his arm around me, I feel most loved by him. He is primarily auditory and has a very strong sense of sound, so when I tell him how much I love him or how handsome he looks and support him in what I say, he is most appreciative.

Maybe you feel that your partner does not express his love for you in the way that you want: he doesn't hug you at the right time or touch you in the right way. But perhaps he loves you in his way. Maybe he takes you out for dinner or finds it easy to give you compliments. If you are someone who is very tactile and you experience love through touch—hugging, sex, cuddling—then you may feel that you are not getting your needs met entirely if your partner expresses his love to you by taking you out for a meal or telling you how much he loves you and yet is not that tactile.

What is your primary sense? How do you feel most loved? Let your partner know this so that he can make more of an effort to express his feelings in the way you understand best.

You may, on the other hand, be in a relationship with someone who is very tactile, but you are someone who experiences being loved when you are given flowers or are taken out for dinner. By discovering what your partner's needs are, you can respond appropriately to them, and in turn by understanding what yours are, your partner can respond effectively to your needs.

What is your partner's primary sense? If he likes to be touched, then hug him more. If he is auditory, then whisper sweet nothings in his ear. If he is more visual, then buy him a small gift or dress up for him. Of course, you could always cover all your bases and do it all!

14 Love the Reality, Not the Fantasy

Did your partner turn out to be the person you always fantasized you would marry? Or is she completely different from the person you envisioned yourself being with? Love your partner for who she is, not for who you thought she would be. It is so easy to wish you were with someone who has every amazing quality, but this fantasy allows you to always find an excuse to not make your marriage work.

Oliver was pretty close to the type of man that I thought I would marry, but once we got married, I had to marry up in the first few months what I had in my head and what I got. I didn't think that I would marry someone who snored so loudly that it was impossible to sleep together. I didn't think I would marry someone who wasn't conscious of what he put into his body. However, I also didn't think that I would marry someone as kind, generous, loyal, warm and forgiving. And I quickly realized that all those other exterior things meant so little in the grand scheme of things and I could easily live with them, because I really got gold!

Maybe you are with someone who doesn't have all the qualities that you were hoping for and, as a result, you find that you are really critical. If that's the case, then it's very likely that your requirements were unrealistic, and that's *your* issue, not hers. These are *your* wounds that you need to heal, not hers. It is very hard for anyone to live up to another person's expectations, and when you have unreasonable expectations, you are setting your marriage up for a fall. Quite often, the kind of person you *thought* you were meant to be with isn't the kind of person you were actually meant to be with at all. So do yourself a favor and pinpoint your partner's five most lovable qualities and give her a break on the less lovable ones!

_____'s Five Most Lovable Qualities:

- - - - - - - - - - - - - - - - - - -   -

- - - - - - - - - - - - - - - - - - -   -

- - - - - - - - - - - - - - - - - - - -

15 Use the Talking Stick

The talking stick is used in many Native American traditions when a council is called. It allows all council members to present their point of view. The talking stick is passed from person to person, and only the person holding the stick is allowed to talk. Everyone else has to listen carefully to what the person with the stick is saying and cannot interrupt. Only when they are given the stick can they speak. In this way, Native American children are taught to listen from age three and also are taught to respect other people's perspectives, even if they don't agree with them.

If you ever talk over each other, if your discussions have a tendency to turn into arguments or if you feel you are not being heard, then the talking stick is an excellent way to communicate and can save enormous amounts of time, energy and heartache within your relationship.

Find a sacred object that can act as your talking stick. Whoever is holding the stick speaks, and the other person has to listen carefully. When the person with the stick is finished (the speaker decides when that is), she gives the stick to the person who has been patiently listening. This person then has the opportunity to speak uninterrupted. Again when the speaker decides that he has finished, he hands the stick back to the first person. The stick goes back and forth until you have each spoken and listened in turn.

If you have problems listening—then use the talking stick method, as it enables you both to be heard. This method can save a lot of marriages, including yours!

16 Don't Dissect the Magic

If your relationship works, don't analyze it too much or try to dissect the magic. The energy between two people cannot be easily defined with human words; that is, within a restricted framework of communication. A relationship is an emotional, spiritual, mental and physical union, and often once you try to break it down, it's no longer mysterious. A relationship is a bit like a magic trick: once you know how the woman is sawed in half, it's no longer enchanting.

You don't have to analyze why or how your relationship is working to know that it is. When two people come together, a "third" entity is created. That mysterious "third" is a composite of both your characteristics, your light and dark, all thrown into a melting pot to metaphysically create a combined extra person in your partnership.

Oftentimes, when you overthink the magic of two people coming together, you can destroy it. So instead of analyzing why your relationship works, trust in the fact that it does and that between you, you have created a working magical and mystical "third."

17 Focus on Your Sex Life

Sex is an important part of every relationship, and having a good sex life is essential to making your relationship work. Sex is the most intimate form of communication we have. If sex isn't working between the two of you, it is rarely because of a physical attraction and chemistry issue and often because you are not communicating well with each other. A lack of sex is a physical manifestation of a lack of communication: it has to do with what you are holding in and have not said to your partner.

Of course you're physically attracted to your partner (or you wouldn't have gotten married!). The best way to keep that chemistry alive is to make sure that you are not holding anything in that you need to say to your partner. However small you think the issue is, you'll find that letting go of it and talking about it will keep you physically connected. Keep being loving, keep giving to your partner, keep talking and remember that you are on a journey together. Make the time to have sex; if you do, you are much more likely to stay close and open with one another always.

18 Hold On to the Invisible Cord

When you marry, there is an invisible, metaphysical cord that goes between you and your partner. And as you go through the ups and downs of life together, you grow and change, but you must always keep a steady hold of your end of the cord. When you argue or disagree, don't in any way, falsely threaten your marriage. Making comments like, "Well, maybe we shouldn't be together, then!" or "Perhaps we should separate!" are big statements and are not to be said flippantly, if deep down you do not believe what you are saying to be true. Comments like this, said out of anger and frustration, strain the cord and unnecessarily put your relationship in jeopardy.

Over time if you keep hold of it, the cord will grow stronger and more stable. You married this person because you love each other. So give to each other, make agreements, say sorry when you need to, forgive each other and be a genuine team. Hopefully, you have a long journey ahead, so hold each other's hand and, above all, hold on to the invisible cord.

19 Practice Tag Team Emotions

Life is full of obstacles, and these ups and downs can either draw you together or tear you apart. Your choice! Your relationship is tested in so many ways and one of the great joys of being in a good marriage is that you don't have to face life's obstacles alone anymore. Playing tag team emotionally can help you strengthen your relationship through difficult times, rather than strain it.

You and your partner are bound to face setbacks—whether it's a loss of a job or parent, or money issues. When a negative incident affects you both, whatever it is, one of you needs to stay strong and hold up the fort. Both of you cannot be too miserable or depressed at the same time. Instead, learn to tag team this strength and weakness so that one of you is always there to help the other.

When my husband lost a job, it was he who had lost it. Even though this had a great impact on me, I had to stay strong for both of us, no matter that it was incredibly hard. We were both sick to our stomachs over it, but he was more so as he was the one who lost the job. I recognized that and put my own feelings aside as much as possible to support him. When we lost a baby at five months, Oli knew that even though he was devastated, I was more devastated than he was, as I was the one who had carried the baby. As a result, he decided to be as strong as he could and support me while I dealt with the grief. And once I had found my footing, he dealt with his feelings in a different way and I was there to support him.

In order to keep your relationship strong during difficult times, you want to tag team your emotions and do your best to assume the different roles, at different times, in order to keep the balance. Sometimes it can be hard to do that, but it's important for the long-term health of the relationship. Your goal during any trying time is to get your lives back on course as quickly as possible, and this balance is essential to making that happen.

Imagine that you are both sitting on different sides of a balanced seesaw—when one person dips down, the other naturally inches up and steadies the other to keep both sides perfectly level. You are always trying to redress that balance and how you get through tough experiences together says a lot about the relationship.

Losing our baby could have torn us apart, but instead it brought us closer together. And when Oli lost a job, it could have taken its toll. Instead, he knew he could lean on me and the experience gave him time to be creative in different ways, develop other skills, bond with our new baby and focus on getting another project off the ground. We came out a stronger family in the end.

20 Remember that the Little Things Count

Much of what makes a marriage happy is not the big things, but how you interact on a day-to-day basis. It's those small acts of kindness that we do for each other daily that really count, more than the grand gestures. Make small gestures, and make them often. To do so, you need to be conscious of the other person at all times and give to him when you are together. One way to do this is to think what you would like him to do for you and then do it for him. Would you like him to hold your hand? Hold his. Would you like him to make you a cup of tea? Make him one. Would you like him to butter your toast? Butter his. Imagine that you are him and step into his shoes; this will help you to become more thoughtful. These small acts of kindness will encourage your partner to give back to you and, as a result, your relationship will benefit from the little things.

21 Be Physically Affectionate

Physical attention is one of the best ways to communicate our feelings because we read each other mostly through our body language. Some studies say it's 55 percent, some say 93 percent, but whatever the exact number is, it is high. Be physical with each other. Touch each other a lot, hold hands and hug. Touching is essential to feeling connected and loved, whether it is taking your partner's hand, putting your arm around her or rubbing her back. Ongoing, daily acts of physical attention are so important.

My parents are wonderful examples of this. They have been together for nearly fifty years and are incredibly physically affectionate with each other. This physical connection helps keep them emotionally connected.

There are many studies that show how important physical touch and connection are for babies; without these, they develop mental, physical and emotional problems. Babies need to be touched a lot and that need does not go away as babies become adults—so make a point to be physically affectionate with each other as much as you can.

22 Share Deeply

Each day find time to be with your partner to emotionally connect and share with him or her in a way that goes beyond the surface of work and kids, even if it's just for ten minutes a day. You need to fill up the emotional well that you share.

If you don't regularly fill up your emotional well, you'll find that your surface communication will become a habit and you'll start to lose sight of each other and even begin to feel lonely within the relationship. One way to recognize that you are not connecting with your spouse is if you find yourself discussing your relationship with your friends, mother, sister and work associate—everyone except the person you really do need to speak about it with, your partner.

Instead, sit down with your partner and take a few moments together at the end of the day to share your feelings. Staying emotionally connected doesn't have to take a lot of time, and it will benefit your relationship in incredible ways.

23 Have Fun Together

In marriage, it's easy to get caught up in the day-to-day responsibilities and lose sight of one of the things that drew you together to begin with—your shared interests and all the fun you have together. Make it a point to play and have fun regularly. What interests or activities do you both like to pursue? You don't need to share everything in common, but shared hobbies can keep you connected and can help sustain your relationship. You need to be best friends and share some activities, whether you like hiking, tennis, playing cards, going to the gym, traveling or playing Scrabble. The healthiest hobbies are those that help you to connect and keep your love relationship alive and kicking.

You might be thinking, *Well, we bring up the kids together* or *We work together,* but that's not what I'm talking about here. I am talking about things that you do that have no stress associated with them and no sense of "having to" do them. These aren't activities that you're obligated to do, but activities that relax you and forge a bond between you, that are fun. Make time to play together, without the children. Create a "no work" zone and keep things simple, light and fun.

24 Listen to Each Other

Oli and I have this game that we play every year on our anniversary. We ask each other questions to see if we were listening to what the other said throughout the year. It started off the first year with questions like these: What was the name of my first dog? What's my favorite color? What was my fish called? And now each year we add new questions: What is the name of the person who cuts my hair? What was my favorite TV show this year? Whose music was I most into this year? We just like to check that we are listening to each other and aware of the little details.

Listening is one of the real foundations of a great relationship. There are many types of listening, but there is only one type that is important to do consistently: it is important to always listen closely to your partner, to the extent that you can recite back to her the exact words that she has used. And when I say exact words, I mean exact. When you use other words to approximate your partner's meaning, even if you think they are similar to what your partner said, you'll find that the meaning inevitably changes in your sloppy translation.

You remember the game of telephone? Well, it's the exact same concept. Someone in the circle starts by whispering something in somebody's ear and that person in turn whispers it in the next person's ear and then that person whispers it in the ear of the next person and so on. By the time the message gets to the tenth person, it isn't even close to what the first person said! So listen intently to your partner's exact words so there's no chance of his or her meaning getting lost in translation.

You also don't want to do the type of listening where you're constantly relating your partner's experience to your own—this shifts your focus from your partner to yourself. You want to be present and to hear what your partner is saying and then repeat back to her what she said, using her words so that she feels heard.

You have two ears and one mouth and I always say to use them in that order, because listening is one of the key components to a successful marriage. When your partner listens to you intently, it encourages you to be more expressive and open and makes for better communication.

25 Fly Separately and Together

Imagine looking up into the sky and seeing two birds flying separately and together in the same direction. That visual image best describes a great marriage. You aren't flying on top of each other, and you aren't leaving the other one behind. You want to be independent from each other, because if you do everything together, it will be very stifling and you will lose your individuality and eventually become resentful. You also don't want to spend too much time apart and give up the time needed to connect. You want to be together and in your own space at the same time.

How do you strike this balance? Give each other the space you need to foster your own interests and relationships. There's nothing wrong with having evenings or weekends apart. In fact, it's really good to let your partner go off and be with friends. A men's or women's weekend away can be very nourishing. No one person can fulfill all your emotional needs, and it's important that you have strong relationships with friends as your partner will never be able to give you everything that you need and expecting him to is asking too much of him. I know that if I have had a week without at least one long, nourishing conversation with one of my girlfriends, I feel a bit low and isolated. My husband needs to spend some time in male company, whether it's going to play golf with a friend, going for a beer or having a long chat with a friend.

Even while it's important to share the same hobbies and interests, it is also very healthy to have separate ones. I enjoy astrology and yoga. My husband's hobby is music. I don't have much of a clue about it, beyond knowing what I like the sound of! (Lucky for him, on car rides he creates the playlist and has complete say over what we listen to.) On the other hand, he knows very little about astrology. In fact, he likes me to discuss astrology with him before going to bed at night as it helps him to fall asleep!

Remember, ladies, men fall more in love with you when you're not there, so when they announce that they want to go on a weekend jaunt with their buddies, bless them on their way. They are going to return more in love with you than ever and, gentlemen, see if I am not correct the next time you go on that golfing or ski trip!

My point is, don't stifle each other, trust that the other one is there for you and give each other space and support for the soul to be expressed.

26 Bring Out the Best in Each Other

You know you are in a good relationship if you both bring out the best in each other. Do you remember in the film *As Good as It Gets* when Jack Nicholson's character tells Helen Hunt's character why he thinks they should be together? He says to her, "You make me want to be a better man." Well, that's what I'm talking about here!

You know when you are with the right person, as you want to be a "better" man or a "better" woman with that person, for him or her. A friend of ours was engaged for a long time in a long-distance relationship. Even though we really wanted our friend, John, to get married, we noticed that the couple really didn't bring out the best in each other. My husband was concerned that John was going to marry: he didn't feel that John wanted to be a "better man" with the woman he had chosen, or she with him. They encouraged each other to drink, smoke and take drugs and we observed that the dynamic wasn't great between them. In the end, they actually did split up.

My husband and I have each found this to be true in our relationship. When I first got together with Oli, he would say that I was very hard on myself. Over time, I started to be kinder to myself, whether that meant going to get a massage, buying a new top or not feeling guilty about watching a movie in the middle of the day, when I felt I needed to be working eight hours a day. He inspired me to be a bit freer and to let go of some of my more rigid patterns because I wanted to make changes for him. And yes, he also changed in many ways.… He no longer lives the wild rock-and-roll lifestyle that he used to have and all that entails. (He said that I am not allowed to give away any more details than that!)

This doesn't mean that you should try to "change" your partner. Rather, we each have incredible capabilities in us and a good relationship will help bring out our very best. Strive to encourage your partner in this way, and let your partner do the same for you.

27 Always Communicate

Communication is key to making your relationship work.

Always communicate so that you don't hold on to issues from the past. If you hold something in—even a small something—it can become magnified over time. Eventually, the issues that you have held in start to add up and layer on top of each other, and before you know it, one brick has become two, then three, then four and so on, until you have built a wall between you both.

Always communicate so that you don't go to bed upset with each other and you can sleep well at night.

Always communicate so that you start fresh with your partner in every moment. If you disagree, let it be only about the current issue being discussed. Do not bring anything up from the past.

Always communicate so that you don't feel the need to get passive-aggressive. This is a sure sign that you haven't been clear and expressive with your partner and that something is bothering you that you haven't discussed. Bring it out into the open and communicate so that you can work it out together.

28 Follow Your Own Rules

Follow your own rules in your relationships and do what is right for you, not what society says is right. As hard as it is sometimes, it is important to ignore what you think society's rules are. Just because society thinks that one way to live or one particular relationship dynamic is correct doesn't mean it's right for you and your relationship.

When Oli and I got together, we realized pretty quickly that we were completely compatible by day and completely incompatible at night. He likes to sleep for a few hours and snores really loudly when he is asleep and I like to sleep for eight hours and I am a very light sleeper. We spent the first six months of our relationship trying every device on the market to stop his snoring and every brand of earplug. Nothing worked and we both suffered from a real lack of sleep. So we decided to sleep separately, and even though society thinks that if you sleep separately, you don't have sex and your relationship doesn't work, we found that the opposite was the case: it enhanced our relationship in every way and we found that we stopped tormenting each other at night. We made our own rule that works perfectly for us.

29 Don't Inspire Nagging

You've probably heard plenty of times that you must "not be a nag," but this tip is a different way to think about the same issue. The whole point is to keep from giving your partner a reason to nag you. If you say you will do something, do it. Don't make your husband or wife ask five times because you have delayed doing it, then call them a nag to deflect the guilt back to them when *you* haven't kept up your end of the agreement. If you didn't want to do what they asked you to in the first place, then you could have said you didn't want to do it. Don't agree to change the oil, pick up your socks, do the dishes, file the taxes—or whatever—if you have no intention of doing it. Figure out a different solution. And if you agree to do something, do it.

30 Expect the First Year to Be a Bit Rocky

Everyone thinks of the first year as the "honeymoon" period, but newlyweds are often dismayed to find that first year to be rockier than they expected. Don't be surprised if your marriage is a little volatile during the first year.

The truth is that the first year tends to be rocky for a few reasons. For one, you are testing each other's boundaries to see how far you can push one another. For another, you are each coming to terms with the disconnect between fantasy and reality, the fantasy idea of who you thought you were going to marry and the actual person you ended up marrying. No matter how much you love your partner, you probably never envisioned how your life would play out on a day-to-day basis. You realize that who you thought you were going to marry and who you did marry in the end are probably pretty different.

The first year of marriage is a reality check. It takes time to build a bridge in your mind between the life partner you'd always fantasized about and the partner who is now in your home. The more quickly you can be more realistic and let go of expectations, the better, because staying in that fantasy place can cause a lot of stress and frustration. The more quickly you can appreciate your partner for who she really is, the better.

Oli and I were much more volatile in our first year of marriage than we are now. I remember arriving in Sri Lanka for our honeymoon. Oli was nursing a headache, his stomach was feeling upset and he had a crook in his neck from sleeping badly. He was walking slowly, almost limping, in front of me because he hurt so much! He had one of his hands supporting his head and the other on his stomach, and I remember thinking, *Oh, shoot, this is who I married?* I had always thought I was going to marry an athlete! Of course there were many things—and *are* many things—that I love about my husband. But at that moment, fantasy and reality collided, and I had to take a minute to readjust my perspective and to remember and appreciate my husband for all his wonderful qualities: the things I love about him that I never would have dreamed up in my wildest fantasies!

31 Mind Your Language

Be careful with the language that you use with your partner as you can easily and unknowingly rub each other the wrong way. Certain language patterns that you may have picked up from your parents or other influences can be damaging to your relationship and anger your partner. Using critical language is not great for your relationship.

Avoid telling your partner that they "have to," "got to" or "should" do something. This language implies that your partner doesn't have any choice, which can really push his buttons as nobody likes to be bossed around or told what to do. You can get the same meaning across using words like "you could" or "you might like to" or "you might choose to" and these will elicit a very different reaction as they give your partner a choice. You'll notice if you become aware of your language and change the way you phrase certain comments, you will get a very different reaction from your partner.

Nobody likes to be bossed around, so be aware of what you want to say, how you say it and how your partner responds. Even if you feel that you are coming from a place of love in terms of what you say, it may not be construed that way, because of the language that you use, your body language and your tone of voice.

Critical Language

Examples: *have to, got to, should*

Body language usually consists of impatient, patronizing gestures, finger pointing and an angry demeanor.

Uncritical Language

Examples: *could, might like to, might choose to*

Body language is attentive, straightforward and nonthreatening.

Test which words bring out the best in your partner and which wind them up, and be sensitive to that when you communicate.

At the same time, unless your partner is highly skilled in language, they may use critical language because they do not know how to say what they want in the most delicate, loving way. If this is the case, you could gently and lovingly tell your partner how it makes you feel and discuss the different choices of words that they may use as well. In that way, you both can communicate with more respect and integrity.

32 Let Go of Being Right

When you're in a disagreement, ask yourself if it's more important to be "right" or to make your relationship work. If it's more important to be "right," then don't be surprised if your relationship doesn't work in the long run. If it's more important to make your relationship work, be prepared to let things go and "lose the battle in order to win the war."

If you look at young children and how they play with each other, their priority is to be happy, not to be right. My son, Judah, can have a scrap with another child and even if the other child is wrong, Judah will let it go quickly because for him it is much more important to be happy than to hold a grudge.

Unfortunately, we often lose sight of this perspective as we get older, but next time you're tempted to hold a grudge because you think "you're right," take a lesson out of a child's book and choose to be happy over your need to be right all the time.

33 Hold Monthly Meetings

Your relationship will grow over time, and you and your partner can work together to create the relationship you both want. How do you envision your marriage in five years, ten years, twenty-five years?

Imagine your marriage is a plane on a journey and you and your partner are piloting the plane from point A to point B. How do you know that you are on track? You, as the pilot, have a course of action and you need to stay as close to that course as possible. Whenever the plane goes off course, you need to check the meter on your panel so that you can see where the plane is and bring it back on course. In the same way, you want to calibrate where you are with your marriage so that you can both keep it on course.

There are many ways to do that and one is to have regular meetings, on a weekly, monthly or quarterly basis. Or maybe even just when you feel you need it. Take half an hour and, without interrupting each other, cover these points. Each of you say:

1. What I love so much about you is…

2. What I love that you have done for me recently is…

3. What I think I could do to improve our relationship is…

4. What I think we could do to improve our relationship together is…

5. What I need in order to become closer to you is…

This way, you can steer the plane back on course before you take too much of a detour—and enjoy the journey along the way, of course!

34 Put Your Partner before Your Kids

Your relationship with your partner must always come before your relationship with your children. Because if your children see that their parents are happy, loving and communicating really well, then they will be happy and feel secure.

The minute you put your children before your spouse, you lose sight of the fact that kids learn mostly by watching what you do and how you and your partner interact rather than by listening to what you say. You and your spouse are partners on each other's journey; your children have their own journey to take without you. Your job is to nurture them and prepare them to fly off from the nest. You are there to give them roots and to give them wings.

If you keep focused on making your marriage great, your kids will be great. When you focus solely on the kids and lose track of your relationship, you run the risk of destroying that essential foundation that children need and will hopefully later replicate. Problems inevitably arise in your relationship and in the family dynamic when you make your kids a priority over each other.

35 Lead (and Follow) by Example

As a couple, you and your partner will grow and change in different ways. Beyond inspiring one another to be better people (see tip #26), through your daily actions and behavior you will have a great influence on one another. Even if you start out with vastly different interests and lifestyles, you will find over time that you come to enjoy many shared interests, because that is how strong an influence you both have on one another.

In a great relationship, the positive aspects of each other's lifestyles will rub off on the other, without either person resisting. Often this can happen without you even noticing. You can be a positive influence on your partner just by leading by example, without criticizing your partner's lifestyle or preaching at her. For instance, I love to exercise and do yoga. Oli never exercised before meeting me, but after seeing how I looked after my body and how I felt so much more relaxed after a yoga class, he decided to follow my example and get in shape. So now he religiously goes to the gym—and I hardly pushed him to do it! And this goes both ways. Oli always made it a priority to stay apprised of the news, while I would spend months on media fasts and have no clue of current events. But because of his influence, the first thing that I read in the morning is the BBC news.

So if you see that your partner is doing something that is good for her mind, body or spirit, do not resist following her on that path for the sake of it. You are together for many reasons and one of them is to open each other's minds and lead by example.

36 Have a Relationship Role Model

To create a great marriage, you need to have at least one role model relationship that you can emulate. Look for a couple who have the same values, who openly love and respect each other, laugh a lot, are really giving, are equals and best friends. Perhaps you'll find a role model in your parents, but that won't necessarily be the case—and it's not necessary. Maybe your grandparents have this kind of relationship, or an aunt and uncle, your friends or even your neighbors.

If you're still stuck, then focus on well-known role model couples. Try to keep away from the smoke and mirrors of the celebrity world, but perhaps you could aspire to a relationship like the Obamas' or even the Gateses'. It's much easier to model yourselves after a couple you know, so the closer to home the better. And all of us, regardless of where we are from, know a relationship that seems to work really well and that we can emulate.

If your parents are happy together, watch and learn how they interact with each other. What works in their relationship that might work in yours? What might you do differently in your relationship? In the same way, if you come from a divorced home, you can learn from your parents' mistakes and figure out what you want to do differently.

My parents are still very happy together, and I personally use some important parts of their relationship as a model for my own. As a child I watched my parents and the way they were together. I noticed that they always put each other first before us; they always spoke from the same song sheet and stuck up for each other, sometimes to our detriment. I hardly ever saw them have big arguments and they were always bolstering each other and telling each other how good they looked.

When I got married, I applied what I loved in their relationship to mine and left out what I wanted to do different. What couple would you want to emulate? And how?

37 Be Mindful of How Your Moods Affect Your Relationship

My husband loves the middle of a quiche and I love the crust. He hates exercise and I love it. He knows everything there is to know about music; I know very little. The fact that you and your partner may have differences really doesn't matter, so long as you feel close despite them—and that feeling of closeness will often depend on your mood.

No doubt, when my husband is in a good mood, he thinks I'm really loyal. When he's in a bad mood, he probably thinks I'm stubborn. When I am in a good mood, my husband is an optimistic person. When I am in a bad mood, I can easily think he is unrealistic. When in a bad mood, my husband probably thinks I am opinionated, and when in a good mood, he might think I'm expressive.

When you are in a good mood, you are more optimistic and lighthearted. You feel closer to your partner and more compatible—it doesn't bother you that you don't share the same taste in music and you appreciate that he lets you have the crust of the quiche. When you are in a bad mood, you are more negative and pessimistic, and you don't feel as close or compatible. Your moods really do shift your perspective. Be mindful of how your mood affects your relationship. Being in the right mind-set will make a huge difference in how you see your partner, and how you interact.

Many years ago I took a fire walking seminar in England, whereby a group of us walked across a twelve-foot bed of white-hot coals. It took hours of training to teach us how to do it and the psychology behind it. When we were all trained, we lined up, ready to go across the path of fire. Just as it was my turn to go, fear overtook me and I scampered to the back of the line to let some other, braver person go before me. The next time I reached the front of the line, fear overtook me once more, and again I "chickened out" and went to the back of the line. The third time in line, I concentrated on shifting my thoughts of fear to excitement, and by the time I got to the front of the line again, I was ready to go. The fire-walking experience was incredible and I was so elated that I walked across the coals again, twice!

In each instance—when I was full of fear and when I shifted to feeling excitement—I had the same physiological symptoms: sweaty palms, an elevated heart rate, a dry mouth, shortness of breath and so on. What was the one major difference? My thoughts. Thoughts always come before a mood, they are what create the mood and what you think can literally change how you feel. In this particular instance, I needed time to literally collect my thoughts and change my perspective.

Excited or frightened? Good mood or bad mood? Your emotions and moods change as a result of your thought patterns. If you are in a good mood, you are going to feel intimate and loving, and think that your partner can do no wrong. If you are in a bad mood, you are more likely to feel at odds, and arguing at that point could be a recipe for disaster.

So think for a second about what kind of mood you are in the next time you want to pick up on something your partner has done or not done, said or not said, and imagine if your response would be different if you were in a good mood. If it would be, then let the matter go for now. Try to hold back and let your negative thoughts and feelings pass, as they always do, and address any issues when you're in a better frame of mind—that way, you're sure to bring yourselves closer together, rather than drive each other apart.

38 Learn about Your Partner

Your partner is hopefully the closest person to you. But how well do you really know him?

Each year you want to take time out to scour through your partner's favorite websites to see what he is reading. Or perhaps you could read one of your partner's favorite books, watch one of his favorite movies or take an interest in one of his hobbies, without needing to take it up yourself. For instance, if your partner is into golf, read a golf magazine. If your partner follows the stock market religiously, learn a bit about it. The more you know about your partner, the closer he is going to feel to you and he is going to be so happy that you made the effort to jump into his world a bit.

One night cook yourselves dinner or go out together and ask each other these twenty questions to test how well you know each other. Each question asks you something about your partner, so take turns asking and answering. This is a fun way to see how well you know your partner and to find out even more about each other!

1. What luxury item would your partner buy for ten thousand dollars?
2. What does your partner worry about most?
3. What is your partner's biggest passion in life?
4. What is your partner best at?
5. What animal does your partner most identify with?
6. If you could buy your partner a car, what kind would he or she like?
7. Who are the three famous people, dead or alive, whom your partner would like to have as dinner party guests?
8. What are your partner's three favorite bands?
9. What are your partner's three favorite movies?
10. If you had to move to a different country, where would your partner want to live?
11. What would be your partner's dream three-course meal?
12. What is your partner's least favorite food?
13. What cause is your partner most passionate about?
14. What are your partner's three favorite books?
15. What was your partner's favorite subject at school?
16. What are your partner's three favorite websites?

17. What is your partner's favorite way of relaxing?

18. What song reminds your partner of when you first met?

19. What was your partner happiest doing as a child?

20. What does your partner value most in life?

39 Don't Argue in Front of the Kids

Do your best not to argue in front of your children. Remember, children soak everything in. Even if you and your partner make up quickly, an argument between the two of you can leave your kids, especially young ones, quite noticeably shaken.

If you feel an argument coming on, do one of two things: step outside of the room and continue it out of earshot of the children or, if that's not immediately possible, put the argument on hold and decide to continue the discussion later.

If your children do see you argue, then disagree with each other in an intelligent way. Keep calm, listen to each other's perspective and dovetail what you both want so that you come to a mutually happy agreement, taking each of your desires into account. By teaching your children that you can disagree respectfully and come to a resolution quickly, you are being a good role model. Remember, your children model their behavior on yours: how you argue is how your children will think it's normal to argue. If you are loud and don't listen to each other, you'll see they will grow up thinking that's normal and will repeat the same pattern in their relationships.

40 Make Unified Decisions

When it comes to children and making decisions about them, do so unanimously so that you come off as one unit. Even if at times you don't agree with each other, never disagree about the children, in front of the children. Instead, discuss the issue among yourselves, away from them. Once you have come to an agreement, you can then tell your children your course of action as a unified front.

Your children will grow up feeling much more secure if they see that you are actively working with one another, as a couple. Even if you sometimes don't make the best decision, it is more important that your child sees that you are acting as one unit. This is one of the most important and influential factors that determine a child's level of confidence. Of course you will disagree with your partner on some parenting methods from time to time, but when this happens, you should work it out together so that you are always on the same page as parents.

41 Address Sleeping Issues

What happens when you and your partner get on wonderfully when you're awake, but terribly when you're asleep? One of you sleeps like a baby as soon as your head hits the pillow and the other snores really loudly or is a bit of a night owl, preferring to pace around at night or watch movies on the internet.

In the first months after meeting my husband, Oliver, I was giddy from the sheer miracle of finding each other and ignored the fact that I was being sleep deprived. However, around the six-month mark, I began to realize that his snoring and sleeping habits were akin to the torture tactics that they use in some prisons.

If you sleep beautifully with your partner, if they are a quiet sleeper, if they don't wake you up ever in the middle of the night and you are wholly compatible while you are asleep, then that's great. But if not, don't despair—you are not alone. Studies estimate that 45 percent of men and 30 percent of women snore on a regular basis and that can lead to huge problems in a relationship, marital disharmony and sometimes even to divorce—and it's not only the non-snorer that ends up not sleeping. Both of you do. Sleep deprivation can leave you both feeling really irritable, unable to think straight during the day and resentful. It's at this point that the bedroom can become a battleground and a place of total disharmony.

For some reason, the "how do you sleep?" subject is a bit taboo and it shouldn't be. There are many solutions that can actually bring you closer together. But first you have to be a bit of a detective to find out what the source of the problem is and determine the remedy that works for you.

If You Snore

First of all, don't deny that you do. If your partner says you do, they're probably not making it up. Instead of being defensive and taking it personally, look for the solution that works for you as quickly as possible.

If you are a selective snorer, that is, you don't snore every night, it might be that you snore when you eat something that you're allergic to for dinner, like dairy. Many people are actually allergic or have a sensitivity to dairy products, but because they don't have an extreme reaction, they are unaware of it. If you find that your nose becomes blocked up after you eat anything with dairy in it, then that means you're having a mild allergic reaction. If so, at night, avoid cheese, butter, creamy desserts, yogurt and ice cream! You can always substitute rice products and see what happens.

Drinking alcohol at night can also really cause snoring. If you can stop, then great. However, if on reading this, your first thought is, *You're crazy. It's completely out of the question!* then try to discover which alcohol makes you snore and how much. You might find that you're fine with a glass of white wine, but not so fine with red wine.

Try to avoid eating a heavy meal within three hours of going to sleep. You could be intolerant to certain foods, which can cause inflammation and a narrowing of the nasal passageways. This can also happen if you are overweight, smoke cigarettes or take prescribed medication.

Experiment to Find a Solution

Once you've ruled out allergies, sleep apnea and breathing problems (consult with a doctor to find out if you have these), then you can experiment with the endless supply of what's available on the market to curb your snoring. Nose sprays, nasal strips, dental devices, throat sprays, mouth guards, pillows and even operations are all options. You are going to have to experiment with different methods and paraphernalia to see what works.

Oli and I travel extensively, and if you asked him, he would joke that because of his snoring he has had the privilege of sleeping in some of the finest hotel corridors and walk-in closets around the world! That is, until we really uncovered the strategy that works for us. A combination of mouth guard, earplugs, nose drops, no dairy, no red wine and a nasal strip.

Now, I couldn't ask him to stick to that regimen every day of his life, because he likes his food and I don't want him to feel restricted and not be himself, so we use this combination when we're away together, and we have a different day-to-day strategy, which brings me to the next suggestion.

Sleep Separately

It's unconventional, but Oli and I have found that sleeping separately has saved our marriage. (See tip #28.) If you and your partner have any form of sleeping incompatibility that is preventing you both from getting the sleep that you need and you think it is affecting your long-term health, then maybe, just maybe, you might want to think about sleeping in separate rooms. Contrary to popular opinion, this by no means signals the end of your sex life, but it does mean that you'll both wake up more rested and happy than you otherwise would. And they do say that absence makes the heart grow fonder....

42 Seek to Understand Rather Than Disagree

In a marriage, it's inevitable that you won't see eye to eye all the time. But you can address these differences of opinion in one of two ways: you can disagree completely or you can seek to understand where your partner is coming from.

When you seek to understand where your partner is coming from, you are opening yourself up to a new way of thinking, and you may possibly even come to the conclusion that your old way of thinking is not necessarily the only way. When you try to understand, you have to open up and discover how your partner thinks and find the place where you can meet in the middle and both agree. In contrast, when you disagree, you are acting critical, arrogant and judgmental by believing that there is only one right way to think—yours. So the next time you and your partner don't see eye to eye on something, seek to understand where the other is coming from, rather than outright disagreeing.

43 Be Supportive through Setbacks

Your partner isn't going to have all aspects of his life put together beautifully at all times, just as you aren't. Life is a journey and a constant balancing act and you are here to help each other as you transform, heal and grow, while being patient and supportive through difficult times.

When your partner experiences a setback, support your partner by letting him know that he is loved and supported by you, regardless, and your partner will do the same for you. It is an honor to be part of another person's journey and to be there to support each other. Be patient and supportive, rather than judgmental, and you can get through difficult times together. Don't panic and wonder what you've gotten yourself into—remember that you married this person for a reason. Trust in that decision, and trust in your partner.

My husband, who has won a British Academy Award as a director and has received many other awards, went through a very difficult time when he moved to America. He did not work consistently for a few years. Oli had always defined himself by his work, and it was very difficult for him when his work flow was inconsistent. It would have been easy enough for me to panic during this time—spotty employment, and we were expecting a baby!—but I didn't. I knew my husband was talented and dedicated and that he'd be on a sure footing again before too long.

Interestingly enough, when he was not working, he grew so much as a person: he became an incredible father, his spiritual life became stronger, he focused on getting healthier and he became creative in other ways. He also realized that his work did not define him. When he did start working again, he did so in an even more mature, creative and confident way as he had evolved so much in the time in between. My point is that our lives are made up of so many different elements, and we have so much to learn and discover about ourselves and so much growing to do in so many different aspects of our lives, whether it is work, relationships, finance, personal growth, health, friendships, family, recreation time and how we contribute to our community, that when we struggle in one area, we may be benefiting in another. So instead of panicking about the aspect of life that isn't working for your partner, support him on his journey and let him grow. Hopefully your journey together will be a long one, and you can hold each other's hand throughout.

44 Don't Be Quick to Blame

Sometimes you or your partner will do clumsy or careless things by mistake. Whether your partner breaks your favorite dish, crashes the car or forgets the passports when going to the airport, these mishaps happen, and as annoying as they are, it is important not to blame (no matter how frustrated you might be) and kick your partner when he is down, so to speak. He knows he messed up; he doesn't need you to add salt to the wound!

This particular aspect of dealing with blame in a relationship became very clear to me when an incident happened with our baby. Oli was putting our baby, Judah, into a sling and he accidentally dropped him and Judah hurt his head on the table. Oli was really upset. He felt terrible. But it was a mistake that anyone could have made. I could easily have given Oli a really hard time about it and yelled at him for being so clumsy and hurting our precious child (it's not easy for any mother to watch her child get hurt). But instead I said to Oli, "Don't worry about it. These things happen." My comment took the air out of the situation. And, not to worry. Judah was better within about three minutes!

It would have been extremely detrimental to our relationship for me to have blamed Oli, and besides, that wouldn't have helped the situation at all. Oli felt awful about it already and I was aware that I could easily have dropped Judah myself. By being relaxed with Oli, he was extremely grateful that his wife supported him rather than blamed him, and I made it clear that we were a team and that these things could easily happen to either of us.

Keep in mind the next time you're tempted to blame your partner for an accident or a mishap that he probably feels awful about already and you'll just be hurting your relationship by laying blame.

45 Deal with Financial Stress

At one time or other in our lives most of us have financial stress. You or your partner may lose a job, lose money or remain unemployed for a long period of time, and making ends meet can become a strain. Money is one of the main causes of arguments in a relationship, and in trying times you don't want to let your financial worries take their toll on your health and your relationship.

Here are just a few ways to help you strengthen your home life and improve your mental well-being in the face of economic uncertainty.

Create a Game Plan

When you do find yourself in a situation where you have to tighten your belt and watch what you are spending, sit down together as a couple and figure out what you are spending your money on. Be clear about how much you have to spend each week and remember not to point the finger at each other or blame each other. You are working as a team to create a game plan that works.

Create a work sheet that details how much money is available to the household each month. Set up a budget for yourselves and prioritize what your needs are and your living expenses and what you can do without. Remember, it doesn't matter who makes the money; you are equal partners and have an equal say in the family finances. You both need to know what is going on and where the money is being spent.

Keep tabs separately and write down what you each spend in a week. Start at the beginning of the week and then compare notes at the end. If you both reach your target, reward yourselves.

Losing a Job

If one of you has lost a job, then you can both brainstorm new ways on how to make money together. Maybe discuss opportunities to get some new career training and take positive steps forward that will help you find another job opportunity.

Look After Your Health

As financial worries can take a toll on your health, make sure that you are conscious of any negative thoughts you have and communicate how you feel. Let go of your anger and resentment that you have. Give each other massages, go on long, relaxing walks, exercise, meditate, take relaxing baths and so on. Remember that worry is not going to help the situation. So once you have put your game plan into action, let go of the stress around it and enjoy other aspects of your life.

Stay Intimate and Loving

Remain intimate and loving with each other. Make sure that you are enjoying a good sex life and are spending really good quality time together. Do your best not to talk about your financial situation all the time that you are together as you do not want it to take over your life; instead set time aside to discuss financial matters and the rest of the time let it go. Take the steps that are needed to change the situation and in the meantime go out and have a good time, as the financial stress will pass.

By staying positive and solving your financial crisis as a team, you will be a great role model for your kids, too. Remember money is important, but your health and your family's harmony are your top priority.

46 Have the End in Mind

It's all too easy to get caught up in the day-to-day things and lose perspective on the bigger picture. To get it back, pick a quiet moment by yourself, sit down, with a pen and paper handy, and fast-forward your life in your mind, imagining that you are really old and that it is the end of your life.

Now reflect on your life and your marriage and replay them in your mind. From this end-of-life perspective, are there any moments in your relationship in which you would have acted or behaved differently? As you imagine remembering your relationship, write down your answers to these ten questions:

1. How could you have been more physical, shown your love more or been more encouraging with your words?

_____

_____

2. How could you have been more thoughtful with your time?

----

3. How could you have been a more considerate listener?

----

4. How could you have enjoyed the moment more with each other?

----

5. How could you have stopped yourself from getting too caught up in your small, day-to-day issues?

_____

_____

6. How could you have made your relationship more fun and exciting?

_____

_____

7. How could you have shared more deeply with each other?

_____

_____

8. What could you have done more of in your relationship and what could you have done less of?

_____

_____

9. What are you happy to have done in your relationship?

_____

_____

10. What actions are you going to take to improve your marriage now?

_____

_____

Perhaps by doing this exercise, you realize that you are completely happy with how you are and you wouldn't change a thing. Maybe you realize that there are things that you would like to address and do differently now so that you don't have regrets later on. It is always good to gain a different perspective. Looking at your relationship as if you are standing outside of it can help you make new decisions on how you are within it.

47 Schedule a Date Night

Just because you're married now doesn't mean you can't—and shouldn't—date your partner anymore. In fact, going out on regular dates with your partner will help keep your relationship strong and ensure that the two of you stay connected. Make sure you have a night out at least once a week, especially when you have kids and nights out alone are harder to arrange.

It doesn't matter how busy you are—there are no excuses, because it's really important to connect as husband and wife. So think of fun things to do. Plan nights away. Arrange for a babysitter if you need to. Dress up for each other and don't skip this really important part of your weekly routine. Relationships suffer when you stop being romantic regularly with each other. So go to a movie, go out for dinner, go out for a drink or do whatever you choose. Just go and be together as lovers.

48 See the Cup as Half Full

There are two ways you can see the world and everything in it—as if the cup is half full, or as if it is half empty. It's particularly important to cultivate a glass-half-full mentality when it comes to your marriage.

Keep focused on what works in your relationship, rather than on what doesn't. If you naturally see the cup as full, then this is going to be natural for you, and if you are a "half-empty" person, then this concept could be a challenge.

To think of it another way: do you spend your time thinking of the problems in your relationship or thinking of the solutions? If you keep thinking of the problems, then you will notice that you have a tendency to analyze and rehash an issue a million times, so it gets bigger and bigger. You will do your best to defend your position and prove that you are "right." (See tip #4.) It is a long, drawn-out, draining process and it is bad for your health to be problem focused. Such an approach can easily cloud the rest of your life and make you feel disempowered.

But problems usually have many solutions, and when you naturally look for solutions instead of fixating on problems, your focus is totally different. You look to build bridges, you keep your mind open for insights and you make way for creative eureka moments, all of which help you to feel empowered. Being a solution-focused person takes being calm and coming to problems with fresh eyes.

So keep focused on what works between you and find solutions where you need to. Keep in mind what you have, not what you don't have. Focusing on problems is being reactive; focusing on solutions is being proactive and keeping the glass half full.

49 Practice Bedroom Feng Shui

The bedroom is where most of us spend at least a third of our lives. It's where we withdraw from the world and rejuvenate as a couple. If we experience a sense of harmony in there, we have a much better chance of coming out into the world in a balanced way, which will, in turn, affect how we go about our day, how much energy we have and how we communicate with others.

Here are nine tips for cultivating harmony in the bedroom:

1. My number one tip for the bedroom is to keep it simple, peaceful and uncluttered. So throw all your old things out and keep it tidy. Make sure that you don't have any excess clothes lying around and make sure that the room is warm and inviting.

2. If you can, don't have anything in there that is too stimulating, such as answering machines, computers and televisions. Nothing should come between you both connecting and sleeping. If you really can't do without your TV in the bedroom, then hide it in a cabinet so that you can't see it all the time

and you can put it away when you're not watching it, rather than having it looming over your sacred space. You don't want to have too many books in your bedroom, either, just one or two that you are reading. This will limit your options and activities so that nothing diverts your attention from the two activities you do want your bedroom for: sex and sleep.

3. If you are going to have photos in your bedroom, make sure they are really happy ones of you both together. It isn't a good idea to have photos up of your parents, siblings or children. It's not exactly sexy having other members of your family staring down at you while you're being intimate.

4. If you want additional pictures or art up in your bedroom, you will want them to contain scenes that relax you. Pictures of nature are the best as they create a sense of peace. Whatever you see in your bedroom needs to be there to enhance your relaxation, rather than stimulate you. So no paintings of battle scenes! Also decorate with colors that relax you. You might want to skip bright red!

5. Put fresh flowers in your bedroom when you can, as flowers stimulate new energy and bring life into the bedroom, or put a plant in the room. The plant will keep the atmosphere fresh, bring life and growth into the area and help lower the toxicity if you have carpets.

6. The best place for the master bedroom is at the back of the house, as the front of the house is where most of the activity takes place, and you want to have your bedroom away from all the comings and goings and activity facing in from the front door. The back right-hand corner of the house is ideal, as that is considered the relationship corner of the house in the Western School of Feng Shui, but the back left corner (the wealth area—see *How Happy Is Your Home?*) is good as well.

7. Make sure the head of your bed is against a wall. This will make you feel secure when you sleep and help you have a good night's rest. Also it is ideal to have a headboard for extra support. And avoid putting your bed against a window, if possible. If you have no choice, then keep the blind down.

8. You also want the widest possible view of the room, and make sure you can easily see the door when you're lying in your bed, as this will give you a sense of being in control. If the only place for the bed is on the same side of the room as the door, then put a mirror up on the wall opposite the door so that when you're in bed, you can easily see reflected in the mirror anyone who comes through the door, without feeling like someone is creeping up on you.

6. This is one of my favorite tips as it always engenders a good discussion: king beds in America are so big that the box spring comes in two pieces, which creates a hidden split in the lower layer of the bed, a feature that can affect your relationship. You can remedy this in a few ways. You can buy a queen-size bed instead, or you can put a red sheet in between the box spring and the mattress, and then imagine the two box springs merging together and visualize your relationship and sex life improving.

50 Expect Your Marriage to Evolve Over Time

A good marriage evolves over time. As the years go on, your relationship may seem to become less stimulating as you become more and more comfortable with each other and open up. But do not worry: what's really happening is that your relationship is going deeper and you are becoming more intertwined.

This sense of feeling relaxed is part of what happens when you are no longer positioning yourself for power but instead are evolving together as a couple. This kind of ease allows you to become more creative and makes it possible for you and your partner to safely evolve and develop as people. It reminds me of the scene in the film *Avatar* when Jake has to find his Declan (flying bird). At first he has to fight the bird, and then once he has made the connection, they become one and fly together in harmony. A relationship is similar: at first there is the jockeying for position and then the relationship goes deeper and relaxes.

When your relationship quiets down, it's easy to get insecure and think that it is not moving forward or is not as good as it once was, but stay chilled about it and refrain from trying to get back what you had in the early stages. Instead, let your relationship evolve. You don't need to see every change under a microscope. If you try to get back what you thought you had in the beginning, it will only lead to frustration, as the initial excitement that you feel in a relationship cannot continue on a long-term basis. Instead, it will come in waves and you will find yourself falling in love with your partner over and over again. You'll probably also notice that you argue less as time goes on, and it becomes much easier to be happier. Most of your thoughts of your partner are positive and you understand each other so much more on a deeper level. Some of you may even feel that sex isn't as important as it was in the first couple of years of being together, as you have learned to be more intimate in other ways that are also important. Over time you'll notice that the person that you married and the person that you are with has evolved and matured, like a fine wine. Just as you have.

SO, HOW HAPPY *IS* YOUR MARRIAGE?

Now it's time to find out how happy your marriage really is—and how you can make it even happier. Take your quiz responses and follow the suggestions below to see which tips are best for you and your relationship.

1. **If you answered:**
   A. See tips: 3, 4, 5, 6, 9, 11, 12, 14, 15, 17, 18, 20, 22, 23, 24, 26, 27, 29, 30, 31, 33, 34, 35, 36, 37, 38, 39, 41, 42, 43, 44, 45, 46, 47, 48, 49
   B. Congrats on having a healthy marriage. Now read on for additional tips to make your marriage even happier.
   C. See tips: 2, 11, 15, 17, 20, 21, 22, 23, 24, 27, 30, 33, 35, 36, 37, 38, 43, 44, 46, 47, 48, 49, 50

2. **If you answered:**
   A. Congrats on arguing effectively. Now read on for additional tips to make your marriage even happier.
   B. See tips: 3, 6, 11, 15, 20, 21, 22, 24, 27, 33, 37, 39, 40, 44, 45, 46, 47, 48, 49
   C. See tips: 3, 4, 5, 6, 7, 12, 15, 17, 18, 20, 21, 22, 24, 27, 30, 31, 32, 33, 37, 39, 42, 43, 44, 45, 46, 47, 48

3. **If you answered:**
   - A. See tips: 13, 15, 17, 22, 27, 30, 31, 33, 44, 47, 49, 50
   - B. See tips: 2, 6, 15, 17, 22, 27, 31, 33, 36, 37, 38, 39, 43, 44, 46, 47, 49, 50
   - C. Congrats on the great level of understanding in your relationship. Now read on for additional tips to make your marriage even happier.

4. **If you answered:**
   - A. See tips: 15, 17, 22, 24, 27, 33, 34, 44, 46, 48, 49
   - B. Congrats on being so open with your partner. Now read on for additional tips to make your marriage even happier.
   - C. See tips: 15, 17, 22, 24, 27, 33, 34, 44, 46, 48, 49

5. **If you answered:**
   - A. Congrats on discussing sex openly with your partner. Now read on for additional tips to make your marriage even happier.
   - B. See tips: 2, 15, 17, 27, 33
   - C. See tips: 2, 15, 17, 27, 33

6. **If you answered:**
   A. See tips: 2, 15, 17, 22, 27, 33, 49
   B. See tips: 2, 15, 17, 22, 27, 33
   C. Congrats on having a desirable amount of sex for both of you. Now read on for additional tips to make your marriage even happier.

7. **If you answered:**
   A. See tips: 2, 15, 17, 33
   B. See tips: 2, 15, 17, 33
   C. Congrats on having a creative sex life. Now read on for additional tips to make your marriage even happier.

8. **If you answered:**
   A. See tips: 15, 25, 33, 46
   B. Congrats on striking the perfect balance. Now read on for additional tips to make your marriage even happier.
   C. See tips: 15, 20, 23, 38, 47

9. **If you answered:**
   A. See tips: 3, 5, 6, 7, 12, 14, 15, 24, 27, 29, 31, 32, 37, 39, 44, 46, 48
   B. See tips: 3, 15, 17, 22, 27, 33, 36, 37, 39, 46, 48

C. Congrats on recognizing when to bring something up and when to let it go. Now read on for additional tips to make your marriage even happier.

10. **If you answered:**
   A. See tips: 3, 4, 6, 7, 11, 15, 18, 22, 24, 27, 29, 31, 32, 37, 39, 42, 46
   B. See tips: 3, 4, 6, 11, 15, 24, 32, 42, 46
   C. Congrats on knowing just how to respond when you've upset your partner. Now read on for additional tips to make your marriage even happier.

11. **If you answered:**
   A. Congrats on knowing how to forgive easily and move on quickly. Now read on for additional tips to make your marriage even happier.
   B. See tips: 5, 11, 12, 15, 27, 32, 44, 46
   C. See tips: 3, 5, 11, 12, 27, 32, 44, 46, 48

12. **If you answered:**
   A. See tip: 9
   B. See tip: 9

C. Congrats on knowing how to handle this awkward situation. Now read on for additional tips to make your marriage even happier.

13. **If you answered:**
    A. See tips: 3, 11, 13, 15, 20, 22, 23, 24, 26, 27, 29, 36, 38, 46, 47
    B. See tips: 2, 13, 17, 20, 21, 46
    C. Congrats on giving a suitable amount to your partner. Now read on for additional tips to make your marriage even happier.

14. **If you answered:**
    A. See tip: 18
    B. Congrats on never resorting to this unhealthy response. Now read on for additional tips to make your marriage even happier.
    C. See tip: 18

15. **If you answered:**
    A. Congrats on knowing how to turn setbacks into opportunities to bring you closer together. Now read on for additional tips to make your marriage even happier.

    B. See tips: 12, 14, 18, 20, 23, 37, 43, 45, 46, 48

    C. See tips: 1, 12, 15, 18, 20, 21, 27, 33, 39, 43, 45, 46, 47, 48, 50

16. If you answered:

    A. See tips: 11, 12, 14, 15, 20, 21, 22, 23, 26, 27, 33, 36, 37, 38, 46, 47, 48

    B. Congrats on exchanging a healthy greeting after a long day apart. Now read on for additional tips to make your marriage even happier.

    C. See tips: 11, 12, 14, 15, 20, 21, 22, 23, 26, 27, 33, 36, 37, 38, 46, 47, 48

17. If you answered:

    A. See tips: 15, 25, 33, 38

    B. See tips: 15, 25, 33, 38

    C. Congrats on knowing when your partner needs some time with his or her friends. Now read on for additional tips to make your marriage even happier.

18. If you answered:

    A. See tips: 3, 4, 5, 6, 7, 10, 12, 13, 14, 15, 17, 18, 20, 24, 25, 26, 27, 29, 32, 33, 35, 46, 49, 50

B. See tips: 3, 4, 5, 6, 7, 10, 12, 13, 14, 15, 17, 18, 20, 24, 25, 26, 27, 29, 32, 33, 35, 46, 49, 50

C. Congrats on bringing out the best in each other. Now read on for additional tips to make your marriage even happier.

19. If you answered:

A. See tips: 13, 14, 23, 24, 26, 33, 35, 38, 46, 47, 48

B. See tips: 13, 14, 23, 24, 26, 33, 35, 38, 46, 47, 48

C. Congrats on having a healthy number of shared interests and hobbies. Now read on for additional tips to make your marriage even happier.

20. If you answered:

A. See tips: 3, 4, 15, 31

B. Congrats on being conscious of your language. Now read on for additional tips to make your marriage even happier.

C. See tips: 3, 4, 15, 31

21. **If you answered:**
    A. Congrats on knowing how to strengthen your bond when the relationship goes off course. Now read on for additional tips to make your marriage even happier.
    B. See tips: 20, 21, 22, 23, 24, 27, 33, 34, 36, 38, 42, 43, 46, 47, 48, 49, 50
    C. See tips: 20, 21, 22, 23, 24, 27, 33, 34, 36, 38, 42, 43, 46, 47, 48, 49, 50

22. **If you answered:**
    A. See tips: 3, 37, 39, 46
    B. See tips: 22, 27, 37
    C. Congrats on keeping a bad day at work from stressing your relationship. Now read on for additional tips to make your marriage even happier.

23. **If you answered:**
    A. See tips: 28, 41
    B. See tips: 28, 41
    C. Congrats on your great sleep compatibility. Now read on for additional tips to make your marriage even happier.

24. **If you answered:**
    A. See tips: 14, 15, 16, 17, 18, 20, 21, 22, 23, 25, 27, 29, 33, 36, 38, 46, 47, 49, 50
    B. Congrats on evolving and growing together. Now read on for additional tips to make your marriage even happier.
    C. See tips: 3, 6, 12, 15, 20, 21, 22, 23, 31, 32, 33, 34, 38, 43, 44, 45, 46, 47, 48, 49, 50

25. **If you answered:**
    A. See tips: 2, 17, 34, 39, 40, 47
    B. See tips: 2, 17, 34, 39, 40, 47
    C. Congrats on knowing how important a weekly date night is.

ACKNOWLEDGMENTS

My deepest thanks to Mum and Dad for being my main example of a great marriage and for being so incredibly supportive, and to Phil and Nick for their love and encouragement.

Thanks to my exceptional editor, Sarah Pelz, and the amazing team at Harlequin, who had the vision and insight to make the *How Happy Is* book brand possible. Special thanks also go to Tara Kelly and Mark Tang for joining forces with the book design, as well as to Shara Alexander and the rest of the marketing team.

Thank you to my warm, wise and supportive literary agents, Shannon Marven, Lacy Lynch, Jan Miller and everyone at Dupree Miller. Your guidance and support have been indispensable.

I must also extend my deepest gratitude to the *Huffington Post,* Babette Perry, Scott Warren, Rebecca and Joel Mandel, Sam Fischer, P.J. Shapiro, Ashley Davis and Andrea Ross. And to everybody at HowHappyIs.com, especially Jon Stout for his endless creativity and Terri Carey for keeping us organized.

And of course, to my husband Oli, and our miracle son, Judah, who is a complete expression of Oli's and my love. Judah, the happiest boy, you rock!

Look for
these other
books in the
How Happy Is
series!

**How Happy Is
Your Love Life?**

**How Happy Is
Your Home?**

**How Happy Is
Your Health?**